AF196108

A Christmas Carol

Charles Dickens

ABOUT YOUR BOOK

📱 Listen to the story and activities
on the HELBLING Media App

💬 Talk about the story

glossary● When you see the red dot,
check the word in the glossary

🅚 Prepare for Cambridge English Exams: A2 Key

FACT FILE Read informative fact files which develop themes from the story

e. Go to **ezone.helbling.com** to do the activities

FOR THE TEACHER

e. Go to HELBLING e-zone for Cyber Homework,
downloadable worksheets, answer keys and
Reading Matters, the Teacher's Guide to using
Helbling Readers in your class.

For a full list of both classic and fiction titles go to
helbling.com/english

Contents

HELBLING DIGITAL

YOUR HELBLING ACCOUNT

Your HELBLING account is the key to the HELBLING digital world: one single login for **HELBLING e-zone** and **HELBLING Media App**.

Registration is easy and available for both teachers and students.

HELBLING e-zone is an easy-to-use interactive learning environment.

Use the **personal access code** on the inside back cover of this book to unlock a host of self-correcting activities, including:

- reading comprehension;
- listening comprehension;
- vocabulary;
- grammar;
- exam preparation.

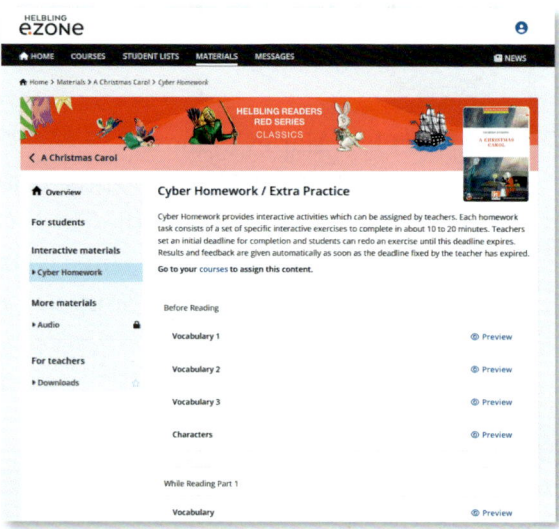

TEACHERS set up classes and assign individual and class homework sets. Results are provided automatically once the deadline has been reached and detailed reports on performance are available at a click. Photocopiable worksheets and answer keys are also available for each HELBLING reader.

STUDENTS test their language skills in a stimulating interactive environment. All activities can be attempted as many times as necessary and full results and feedback are given as soon as the deadline has been reached. Single student access is also available.

INTERACTIVE TEACHING
AND LEARNING MATERIALS

HELBLING Media App

Quick access to multimedia material at any time, anywhere – with or without an internet connection.

The full audio is available via the **HELBLING Media App** for both students and teachers, on mobile devices and desktop computers.

The **HELBLING Media App** is available for free for Android, iOS, Windows and macOS.

Download from the app store of your choice or via **helbling.com/media-app**

FOR TEACHERS

helbling.com/readersblog

Love reading and readers and can't wait to get your class interested?

Have a class library and reading programme, but not sure how to take it a step further?

The HELBLING Readers Blog is the place for you.

Here you will find:

- interviews;
- book club tips;
- calendar;
- lesson plans.

ABOUT THE AUTHOR

Charles Dickens was one of Britain's most popular writers. He was born in Portsmouth, in the south of England, in 1812, the second of eight children. The family moved frequently because of his father's work as a clerk• in the Navy• and Dickens did not have a steady• education, although he loved reading and spent a lot of time out of doors. Dickens's father did not earn• enough to support his family, and when Dickens was twelve, his family were sent to a debtors' prison•. Dickens started working in a factory•. Throughout his life, he did his best to stop the suffering• of the poor, especially children.

As a young man, Dickens found work as a journalist and came into contact with a number of people. He enjoyed writing descriptions of the people he met. He wrote about the difficulties of life, as well as its funny side. Soon, Dickens started writing stories that he published in monthly instalments•. His first novel, *The Pickwick Papers,* had only a small following• at first, which went up to 40,000 copies per instalment! Dickens was a prolific• author, and among his most famous works are *Great Expectations*, *A Christmas Carol•*, and *Oliver Twist*.

Dickens's work introduced readers to a new type of novel which used fiction to talk about the most important social problems of the period. Charles Dickens died in 1870.

GLOSSARY

- **carol:** song sung at Christmas time
- **clerk:** person who works in an office
- **debtor's prison:** prison for people who owed money
- **earn:** get money for working
- **factory:** building where things are made
- **following:** (here) people who read it
- **instalments:** parts
- **Navy:** people who fight for their country at sea (on boats)
- **prolific:** who wrote a lot
- **steady:** constant
- **suffering:** great pain

ABOUT THE BOOK

London, at the beginning of the 19th century, was the largest city in the world, and it was crowded•, dirty and dark. There was great poverty in the city, and many adults and children had to work very long hours in very bad conditions.

Charles Dickens spent most of his life in London. And the descriptions of the city in his books allow readers to experience the sights, sounds and smells of the old city.

The main theme in *A Christmas Carol* is, of course, Christmas. However, at the beginning of the Victorian period, nobody really celebrated Christmas. People didn't have enough time; they had to work hard.

During the Victorian period, people began to sing Christmas carols again. Prince Albert, Queen Victoria's husband, introduced the German tradition• of decorating Christmas trees. And the first Christmas card appeared in the 1840s. But it was the Christmas stories of Charles Dickens, particularly his 1843 story *A Christmas Carol,* that brought the joy of Christmas to Britain and America. People associated the name of Dickens with Christmas. On hearing of his death• in 1870, many children said, "Mr Dickens dead? Then will Father Christmas die, too?"

Today, *A Christmas Carol* continues to be relevant•. It sends the message that Christmas is a time to think about other people. It's a time to forgive•, and a time to be generous.

- **crowded:** with too many people
- **death:** end of life
- **forgive:** pardon
- **relevant:** important
- **tradition:** something people have done or believed for a long time

Child workers in Dickens' time

Childhood
in DICKENS

In *A Christmas Carol,* we meet Tiny Tim, one of Dickens's best-loved characters. Tiny Tim is a suffering child, and he represents all the innocent, abused, abandoned, or simply neglected• children that populate Dickens's novels. Many of them are orphans in a seemingly• indifferent society.

The creation of characters such as Tiny Tim, Oliver Twist, David Copperfield and Pip (in *Great Expectations*), shows Dickens's concern• with children and their fate• in Victorian England. He clearly wanted to encourage deeper social awareness• about children's problems. He thought that they deserved special care to protect them from hardship•, hunger and separation from their families. His concern reflected the growing attention given to children in the nineteenth century, especially in Britain. This century was characterized, among other things, by the development of a new idea of the child. Before this, society considered children to be uninteresting, or incomplete adults. By Dickens's time, however, this idea was changing, and children were seen more objectively, and even as being closer to mankind's• original, natural state.

Children in factories

Factory owners employed children because they were cheap, had lots of energy and they did not complain•. Because they were small, they could do very detailed work and also crawl• under machines to fix broken parts. In 1874, a law called *The Factory Act* said that children under 10 could not work in factories.

Dickens and factories

Dickens's idea of children reflected his own terrible experiences as a child: his father was arrested for bankruptcy when he was twelve, and Dickens had to leave school and work at a factory making shoe polish•. These experiences returned again and again in his fiction. Dickens himself writes in an autobiographical fragment•, "all these things have worked together to make me what I am."

Did you know?

Dickens was a very affectionate parent when his ten children were very little, but then he gradually became harder and more distant when they grew up.

GLOSSARY

- **awareness:** knowledge
- **complain:** say what made them unhappy
- **concern:** worry
- **crawl:** move on their hands and knees
- **fate:** destiny; future
- **fragment:** small piece (here, of writing)
- **hardship:** difficult situations
- **mankind:** people; everybody
- **neglected:** not given enough care or attention
- **seemingly:** that seems
- **shoe polish:** cream for cleaning shoes

The young Dickens in the shoe polish factory by Fred Barnard

A Christmas Carol

Ebenezer Scrooge

The Ghost of Christmas Yet To Come

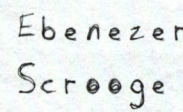

Marley's Ghost

Scrooge as a boy

The Ghost of Christmas Past

The Ghost
of Christmas
Present

Belle

Screoge
as a young man

Screoge's
nephew

Tiny Tim

Bob
Cratchit

11

BEFORE READING

1 **What does the title tell you about the book?**

2 **Look at these pictures from the book and guess the answers to complete the statements.**

  a The story takes place in
    1 ☐ the past.
    2 ☐ the present.
    3 ☐ the future.

  b The story takes place in
    1 ☐ Paris.
    2 ☐ London.
    3 ☐ New York.

3 **Describe the city in the picture. Would you like to live there?**

4 Match the words to the photos. Find the words in the story.

a candle   **b** torch   **c** coal scuttle   **d** door knocker
e keyhole   **f** bedpost   **g** crutches   **h** gravestone

1    **2**    **3**    **4**

5    **6**    **7**    **8**

 ## 5 Listen and number.

a

b

c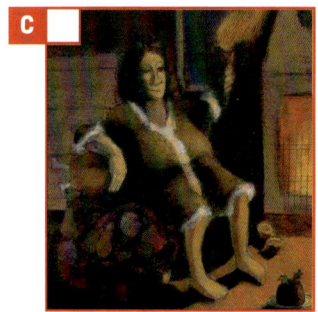

d

BEFORE READING

1 Read the description of Christmas in Charles Dickens's time. Write the numbers in the pictures.

*We have a lot of parties at Christmas time. Christmas is a time to be with family and friends. It is a time to think about other people. We give presents to our family and friends and we give money to the poor. We decorate our houses with **(1)** holly and **(2)** mistletoe. I love the red berries on the holly.*

*In the afternoon, we have a big family dinner and we eat a roast **(3)** turkey. For dessert, we have **(4)** Christmas pudding. It is a big round cake made with dried fruit and we eat it hot. We also eat **(5)** chestnuts and **(6)** mince pies. Mince pies are small pies filled with dried fruit.*

2 How do you celebrate Christmas? Tell a partner, then together write a short description of Christmas in your country or area.

3 In the story, you meet the **Ghost of Marley**. Label the ghost with the words in the box.

| cash-box | bandage | chain | keys | padlock |

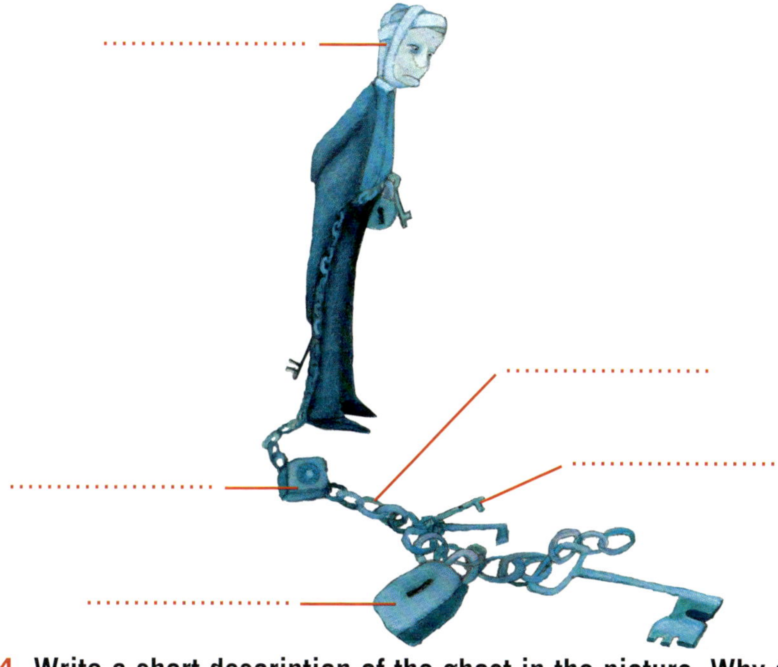

....

....

....

....

....

4 Write a short description of the ghost in the picture. Why do you think he has appeared? What is the meaning of the things attached to him?

5 Are you afraid of ghosts? What are you afraid of? Tick (✓) below, then compare with a partner. Talk about a frightening experience you had.

☐ bullies   ☐ dogs
☐ ghosts   ☐ lifts
☐ spiders   ☐ storms
☐ teachers   ☐ the dark

I have tried to write a ghost story that won't make you unhappy with yourselves, with each other, with the season, or with me. I hope it haunts your houses pleasantly*.*

Charles Dickens

PART I: MARLEY'S GHOST

MARLEY was dead. There is no doubt* about that. The clergyman*, the clerk*, the undertaker*, and the chief mourner* signed the register at his funeral. Scrooge signed it. Old Marley was as dead as a door-nail*.

Did Scrooge know he was dead? Of course he did. Scrooge and he were business partners for years. Scrooge was his only friend, and his only mourner.

Scrooge was a cold, greedy, mean old man! The cold within him froze* his old face. It made his eyes red, and his thin lips blue. And it spoke out in his unkind voice. A frost* covered his head, his eyebrows, and his pointed chin. He iced his office, and he didn't thaw* it one degree at Christmas.

GLOSSARY

- **chief mourner:** friend or relative of the dead person
- **clergyman:** religious leader
- **clerk:** person who works in an office
- **dead as a door-nail:** expression meaning definitely dead
- **doubt:** uncertainty
- **frost:** covering of ice
- **froze:** stopped it from moving
- **haunts:** visits (of a ghost)
- **pleasantly:** in a friendly, nice way
- **thaw:** make ice melt
- **undertaker:** person who organises funerals

17

Nobody ever stopped Scrooge in the street to say, 'My dear Scrooge, how are you?' No beggars• asked him for a penny. No children asked him, 'What time is it?' No man or woman ever asked Scrooge for directions. And dogs ran away from him.

Once upon a time, on Christmas Eve, old Scrooge sat in his office. It was a cold foggy day. He could hear the people outside, stamping• their feet on the pavement to warm them. It was only three o'clock, but it was already quite dark. The candles were flickering• in the windows of the neighbouring• offices. The fog poured in• through every keyhole•. It was so thick that the houses opposite were merely• ghosts.

The door of Scrooge's office was open. He wanted to keep his eye on his clerk, Bob Cratchit. Bob sat in a cold gloomy• little cell•. He was writing letters. Scrooge had a very small fire, but Bob's fire was even smaller. Bob couldn't add any more coal•, because Scrooge kept the coal scuttle• in his room. So Bob put on his white woollen scarf and tried to warm himself by the candle.

GLOSSARY

- **beggars:** poor people asking for money or food
- **cell:** very small room, like a prison
- **coal:** black mineral used in fires
- **coal scuttle:** object to keep coal
- **flickering:** (of light) moving
- **gloomy:** dark and unwelcoming
- **keyhole:** place to put keys in a door
- **merely:** no more than
- **neighbouring:** next door
- **poured in:** a lot came in quickly
- **stamping:** putting down heavily

BOB CRATCHIT

Imagine you are Bob Cratchit.
Describe your feelings.

'A Merry Christmas, Uncle!' cried a happy voice. It was Scrooge's nephew.

'Bah!' said Scrooge. 'Humbug•!'

'Christmas a humbug, Uncle!' said Scrooge's nephew. 'You don't mean that, I'm sure.'

'I do,' said Scrooge. 'Merry Christmas! What reason have you got to be merry? You're poor.'

'OK, then,' replied his nephew, cheerfully. 'What reason have you got to be sad? You're rich. Don't be cross, Uncle!' said his nephew.

'What else can I be?' replied Scrooge. 'I live in a world of fools•. Merry Christmas! What's Christmas time to you? It's a time for paying bills• without money. It's a time for finding yourself a year older, but no richer. Every fool who says "Merry Christmas",' said Scrooge, 'should be boiled• with his own Christmas

GLOSSARY

• **bills:** letters asking for money you must pay
• **boiled:** cooked in water
• **fools:** stupid people
• **humbug:** (here) hypocrite (empty words)

20

pudding. Then, he should be buried with a stake of holly through his heart!'

'Uncle!' begged the nephew.

'Nephew!' replied Scrooge. 'Celebrate Christmas in your own way, and let me celebrate it in mine.'

'Celebrate it!' repeated Scrooge's nephew. 'But you don't celebrate it.'

'Let me leave it alone, then,' said Scrooge. 'What good has it ever done you?'

'Uncle,' said Scrooge's nephew, 'I have always thought of Christmas time as a good time, a kind, charitable, happy time. And so, Uncle, although Christmas has never put any gold or silver in my pocket, I think it has done me good. And it will do me good. And I say, God bless it!'

CHRISTMAS

What is Christmas time to you?
What do Scrooge and his nephew think of Christmas?
Do you agree with Scrooge or with his nephew?
Give reasons.

- **begged:** (here) said with emphasis
- **buried:** put under the ground
- **charitable:** helpful and generous

- **holly:**
- **stake:** wooden stick with a sharp end like a knife (used to kill Dracula)

21

The clerk in the cell applauded•. Then realising his mistake, he poked the fire•. And he put out• the last little spark• forever.

'One more sound from you, Bob Cratchit,' said Scrooge, 'and you'll celebrate Christmas by losing your job!' Then, he turned to his nephew and said, 'You're quite a powerful• speaker, sir. I'm surprised you don't become a politician•.'

'Don't be angry, Uncle. Come and have dinner with us tomorrow.'

'No,' said Scrooge.

'I'm sorry you don't want to celebrate Christmas. But, I do. So, a Merry Christmas, Uncle!'

'Good afternoon!' said Scrooge.

'And a Happy New Year!' said his nephew.

'Good afternoon!' said Scrooge again.

His nephew left the room. He stopped to wish Bob a Merry Christmas. And Bob replied, 'A Merry Christmas to you, too.'

GLOSSARY

- **applauded:** clapped his hands
- **poked the fire:** moved the coals to make the fire burn better
- **politician:** person whose job is politics, governing a country
- **powerful:** strong; good
- **put out:** stopped burning
- **spark:** (here) very small flame or light

'There's another fool,' muttered Scrooge. 'My clerk, with only fifteen shillings• a week, and a wife and family, is talking about a Merry Christmas!'

• **muttered:** talked quietly (usually when angry or complaining)

• **shillings:** old British money

As Scrooge's nephew left, two kind old gentlemen came in. They stood in Scrooge's office.

'Scrooge and Marley's, I believe,' said one of the gentlemen, looking at his list. 'Have I the pleasure of talking to Mr Scrooge or Mr Marley?'

'Mr Marley died seven years ago, this very night,' Scrooge replied.

'We are sure that you will be just as generous• as he was,' said the gentleman.

Scrooge certainly was. Scrooge and Marley were as mean as each other. At the word "generous", Scrooge frowned• and shook his head.

'At Christmas time, Mr Scrooge,' said the gentleman, picking up a pen, 'we should give to the poor. They really suffer• at this time of year. They have no shelter• or food, sir.'

'Are there no prisons•?' asked Scrooge.

'There are plenty of prisons,' said the gentleman, putting the pen down again.

'And the workhouses?' continued Scrooge. 'Are they still in operation•?'

GLOSSARY

- **frowned:** looked angry
- **generous:** kind; giving a lot of money or help
- **in operation:** working; in use
- **prisons:** buildings for criminals
- **shelter:** place to stay
- **suffer:** feel pain or unhappiness

'They are,' replied the gentleman, 'but I wish they were not.'

'Good,' said Scrooge. 'I'm very glad to hear it.•'

'We don't think that workhouses do enough for people,' replied the gentleman. 'So we are trying to raise money• to buy the poor some clothes and some food at this special time of year. What shall I put you down for•?'

- **I'm very glad to hear it:** that is good news
- **raise money:** collect money for a person or thing

- **What shall I put you down for?:** How much do you want to give?

'Nothing!' Scrooge replied. 'I give some money to the prisons and the workhouses. That's enough. The poor must go there.'

'Many people can't go there. And many people prefer to die than to go there.'

'Then let them die,' said Scrooge. 'There are too many people in the world anyway. Good afternoon, gentlemen!'

The gentlemen left. And Scrooge felt very pleased with himself•.

WORKHOUSES

Workhouses in Victorian England were places that people with no house or money could stay in. The conditions in the workhouses were very bad. Husbands and wives had to live separately• and parents couldn't see their children. Many people preferred death• to these places. Charles Dickens describes them in many of his novels. Find out more about them online.

GLOSSARY

- **death:** end of life
- **decorated:** made nicer
- **felt very pleased with himself:** was happy with his actions
- **grew thicker:** there was more fog
- **separately:** apart; not together
- **shivering:** moving quickly with cold

Meanwhile, the fog grew thicker•, and it grew colder and darker. But the shops were brightly lit and decorated• with holly. Everybody was preparing for Christmas.

A boy, shivering• with cold, began to sing a Christmas carol at Scrooge's keyhole. But when Scrooge heard the boy sing, 'God bless you, merry gentleman!', he picked up his ruler and banged the door. And the boy ran away, leaving the keyhole to the fog and frost.

At long last•, it was time to shut the office. Scrooge got down from his stool and told his clerk to leave the gloomy cell. The clerk immediately blew out his candle and put on his hat.

'You'll want the whole• day off tomorrow, I suppose•?' said Scrooge.

'Um, if it's all right, sir.'

'It's not all right,' said Scrooge, 'and it's not fair•. I have to pay you a day's wages• for no work.'

'It's only once a year!' said the clerk.

'Well, make sure you get here early the next morning,' muttered Scrooge.

The clerk promised to be early, and Scrooge walked out with a growl•. Quickly, the clerk closed the office. Then he ran home to Camden Town.

Scrooge lived in Jacob Marley's old apartment. It was very rundown•. And it was so gloomy that nobody else wanted to live there. The rest of the rooms were offices.

GLOSSARY

- **at long last:** finally
- **fair:** right
- **growl:** angry sound (usually made by dogs)
- **rundown:** old and in bad condition
- **suppose:** guess; think
- **wages:** money given for working; salary
- **whole:** all; complete

That evening, the fog and frost hung over the black gateway to the house. And the yard was so dark that Scrooge had to feel his way● along with his hands.

Now, there was nothing strange about the knocker● on the door of the house. Scrooge saw it every night and every morning. But tonight, when Scrooge put his key in the lock, he saw Marley's face instead of the knocker.

It was definitely Marley's face. Scrooge stared at the face. And it became a knocker again.

Scrooge was scared, but he put his hand on the key again. He quickly turned it. Then he walked inside and lit a candle. After that, he closed the door with a bang.

● **feel his way:** touch in order to be sure of the way

● **knocker:** metal object on a door (see picture)

The sound echoed• through the house like thunder•. But Scrooge was not frightened by echoes. He locked the door and walked across the hall and slowly up the stairs.

It was very dark because Scrooge only had a candle. But darkness didn't worry Scrooge. Darkness is cheap•, and Scrooge liked cheap things. But before he shut the heavy door of his apartment, he looked in every room.

There was nobody in the sitting room or the bedroom. Scrooge closed his door, and then locked it. Then he took off his cravat• and put on his dressing-gown• and slippers•. Finally, he sat down in front of the fire to eat his gruel•.

GLOSSARY

- **cheap:** not expensive
- **cravat:** neck tie men wore in the past
- **dressing-gown:** long piece of clothing worn over night clothes
- **echoed:** was heard again and again
- **gruel:** food which poor people ate (made by boiling oats in water or milk)
- **slippers:** soft indoor shoes
- **thunder:** very loud sound heard in a storm

Suddenly, he heard a loud clanking• sound. It came from downstairs. Somebody was pulling a heavy chain• over the barrels• in the wine merchant's• cellar•.

The cellar door flew open with a bang. Then the clanking sound became much louder. It came up the stairs. It was coming straight towards his door.

'Humbug•!' said Scrooge. 'I don't believe it.'

- **barrels:** large round containers for food or liquid
- **cellar:** room below ground
- **chain:** rope made of metal rings
- **clanking:** when two metal objects hit each other
- **Humbug!:** (here) nonsense!
- **wine merchant:** man who buys and sells wine

But then, to his horror•, it came straight through the heavy door. And it passed into the room. The face was the same. It was Marley. He was dragging• a chain. It was long, and moved behind like a tail. Steel• cash-boxes, keys, padlocks and heavy purses hung from the chain. Scrooge stared at the Ghost of Marley as it stood there before him. He felt a chill• from its death-cold eyes. He saw the bandage around its head and chin. But still he didn't believe it was really there.

'Who are you?' asked Scrooge, calmly.

'Ask me who I was.'

'Who were you then?' said Scrooge.

'In life, I was your partner, Jacob Marley.'

Scrooge was trying very hard not to be scared. The Ghost's voice scared him, and its cold eyes frightened him. Then the Ghost took off the bandage from its head. And its lower jaw• dropped down onto its chest! Scrooge was horrified•.

Scrooge fell to his knees. 'Mercy•!' he said. 'Why have you come?'

'Do you believe in me or not?' asked the Ghost.

'I do!' said Scrooge. 'I must!'

GLOSSARY

- **chill:** cold fearful feeling
- **dragging:** pulling with difficulty
- **horrified:** very shocked
- **horror:** shock
- **jaw:** bones around the mouth
- **mercy:** be kind and understanding
- **steel:** hard metal

The Ghost cried out. It shook• its chain. And it wrung• its shadowy• hands.

'Why are you carrying that chain?' asked Scrooge, trembling•.

'I wear the chain that I made in life,' replied the Ghost. 'I made it link by link, and metre by metre. I wound it around myself. Does it look strange to you?'

Scrooge trembled more and more.

'Would you like to feel the weight of the chain you are carrying?' continued the Ghost. 'It was as heavy and as long as this, seven Christmas Eves ago. You have worked very hard on it, since. It is a huge• chain now!'

Scrooge looked at the floor around him. But there was no chain. 'Jacob,' he cried. 'Old Jacob Marley, explain everything to me!'

THE CHAIN

Marley's chain is symbolic. What is it a symbol of?

a ☐   The things that are important in life.

b ☐   The things that were important to Marley when he was alive.

c ☐   The things that Marley forgot when he was alive.

GLOSSARY

- **huge:** very big
- **shadowy:** like a ghost
- **shook:** moved quickly from side to side
- **trembling:** shaking/moving with fear and shame
- **wrung its hands:** twisted its hands round and round in unhappiness

'I can't,' the Ghost replied. 'I can't stay long. I have to travel all the time! I can't rest. I can't stay anywhere.'

'You have been dead for seven years,' said Scrooge, 'Have you been travelling the whole time?'

'Yes, the whole time,' said the Ghost. 'No rest, no peace!' The Ghost of Marley cried again. And it clanked its chain. 'I had the opportunity to be kind and do good in life. But I did nothing. And now I'm dead, I regret● that!' cried the Ghost.

'But you were always a good businessman, Jacob,' said Scrooge.

'Business!' cried the Ghost, wringing its hands again. 'The welfare● of mankind● was my business. Charity, kindness, and generosity were all my business. My job was only a drop of water in the huge ocean of my business!'

- **mankind:** people; everybody
- **regret:** feel sorry that he did/didn't do something

- **welfare:** good health and happiness

MARLEY

The Ghost of Marley says his job was "a drop of water in a huge ocean". What does he mean here? It is a metaphor. Can you find any more metaphors in the story? Look for them while you are reading.

The Ghost held up its chain. Then it flung• the chain heavily on the ground again.

'At this time of year,' the Ghost said, 'I suffer most. Why did I ignore• the suffering and poverty• around me, when I was alive•?'

Scrooge was very upset• to hear the Ghost talking like this.

'Listen to me!' cried the Ghost.

'I will,' said Scrooge. 'But please don't be hard on me, Jacob!'

'I don't know why I am visible• to you now. I have sat invisible beside you many times.'

It was not a nice idea. Scrooge trembled at the thought of it.

GLOSSARY

- **alive:** living
- **flung:** threw
- **ignore:** take no notice of
- **poverty:** state of being poor
- **upset:** unhappy
- **visible:** something you can see

'I'm here tonight to warn• you. You can still escape my fate•. I'm giving you a chance, Ebenezer,' continued the Ghost.

'You were always a good friend to me,' said Scrooge. 'Thank you!'

'Three ghosts will come and haunt you,' continued the Ghost.

Scrooge's jaw fell almost as low as the Ghost's. 'I – I don't want them to come,' he said.

'Without their visits,' said the Ghost, 'you can't avoid• my fate. The first will come later, when the clock strikes• one.'

'Can't I see them all at once, Jacob?' pleaded• Scrooge.

'The second will come on the next night at the same time. The third ghost will come just after the second one. You won't see me again, but remember my words!'

The Ghost took its bandage from the table, and wound• it around its head again. Then the Ghost walked backwards away from Scrooge. And at every step it took, the window opened a little. When the Ghost finally reached the window, it was wide open•.

Scrooge heard voices crying outside. After listening for a moment, Marley's Ghost started crying, too. Then it floated• out into the dark night.

- **avoid:** do something to stop another thing from happening
- **fate:** destiny; future
- **floated:** moved slowly through air
- **pleaded:** asked in a strong and serious way
- **strikes:** (here) rings
- **warn:** tell a person about a danger before it happens
- **wide open:** completely open
- **wound:** wrapped/put around

Curious•, Scrooge followed the Ghost to the window and looked out. The sky was full of ghosts. All of them wore chains like Marley's Ghost. Scrooge recognised many of them. There was one old ghost in a white waistcoat•. Scrooge knew it quite well. It had a huge metal safe• attached to its ankle. And it cried because it couldn't help a poor woman and her child, sitting in the street below. The ghosts were all miserable• because they wanted to help the people below. But now they were dead, they couldn't help them.

Then the spirit• voices faded•. Scrooge closed the window. He felt very tired so he went straight to bed.

GLOSSARY

- **curious:** interested; wanting to know
- **faded:** became quieter and quieter
- **miserable:** unhappy
- **safe:** strong box for money and jewellery
- **spirit:** ghost
- **waistcoat:** jacket without sleeves

PART II: THE FIRST OF THE THREE GHOSTS

When Scrooge woke up, it was very dark. A clock struck twelve! Scrooge suddenly remembered, *Another ghost is coming at one o'clock.* He decided to lie awake until after one o'clock.

He waited and waited, until at last he heard the clock strike one. At that moment, a light flashed° in the room. And the curtains round his bed flew open°.

Scrooge sat up, and found himself face to face° with a ghost.

It was very strange. It was the height of a child, but it looked like an old man. Its long hair was white like an old man's, but there were no wrinkles° on its face. It wore a white tunic. And a bright jet° of light beamed° out from the top of its head. It held a big cap under its arm.

- **beamed:** shone; came out of
- **face to face:** looking at
- **flashed:** shone suddenly
- **flew open:** opened quickly and suddenly
- **jet:** strong thin line
- **wrinkles:** lines on people's faces showing age

'Are you the ghost that Marley told me about?' asked Scrooge.

'I am!'

'Who are you?' Scrooge continued.

'I am the Ghost of Christmas Past.'

'Why have you come?' asked Scrooge.

'For your welfare!' said the Ghost. 'Now, stand up and walk with me!'

When Scrooge saw the Ghost move towards the window, he was frightened. 'I'm a mortal,•' said Scrooge, 'I'll fall.'

The Ghost laid• its hand on Scrooge's heart and said, 'You won't fall!'

As it spoke, they passed through the wall. And they stood on a country road. There was no mist• or darkness now. It was a clear, cold winter's day. And there was snow on the ground.

'Good Heavens•!' said Scrooge, as he looked about him. 'I grew up• here. I was a boy here!'

They walked along the road. And Scrooge recognised every tree and every gate. Some ponies• were trotting• towards them with boys on their backs. All these boys were happy and shouting to each other.

GLOSSARY

- **Good Heavens!:** expression of surprise
- **grew up:** (here) passed my years as a child
- **laid:** placed; put
- **mist:** fine vapour like a low cloud
- **mortal:** person; human (can't live forever)
- **ponies:** small horses
- **trotting:** (of a horse) moving

'They are only shadows,' said the Ghost. 'They can't see us.'

Scrooge knew all the boys. But why was he so happy to see them? Why was he happy when they called Merry Christmas to each other? What was Merry Christmas to Scrooge? *What good has it ever done me?* he asked himself.

'The school is not quite empty,' said the Ghost. 'One child is still there.'

'I know,' said Scrooge, with a tear• in his eye.

They soon came to a large red-brick• building. They entered the gloomy hall and walked to a door at the back of the building. It opened before them, and they saw a long empty classroom. At one of the desks, a lonely boy was reading a book. Scrooge sat down on a bench and wept• when he saw himself.

'I wish,' Scrooge muttered, after drying his eyes with his sleeve•, 'but it's too late now.'

'What's the matter?•' asked the Ghost.

'Nothing,' said Scrooge. 'There was a boy singing a Christmas carol at my door last night. I would like to give him some money. That's all.'

The Ghost smiled thoughtfully, and said, 'Let's see another Christmas!'

GLOSSARY

- **red-brick:**
- **sleeve:** arm of a shirt, jumper or coat
- **tear:** water from one's eye when one cries
- **wept:** cried
- **What's the matter?:** What is the problem?

42

THE BOY

Who do you think the boy is?
Why does Scrooge cry?

They left the school behind them, and a moment later, they were in a busy city. It was Christmas time again, but it was evening.

The Ghost stopped at a warehouse• door.

'Do you recognise this place?' asked the Ghost.

'I was an apprentice• here!' said Scrooge.

They went in. Scrooge saw an old gentleman sitting behind a high desk. 'It's old Fezziwig!' he said, excitedly. Old Fezziwig rubbed his hands• and laughed. Then he called out in a rich, fat, cheerful• voice, 'Ebenezer! Dick!' Scrooge's former self•, now a young man, came quickly into the room, with Dick, the other apprentice.

'Dick Wilkins!' said Scrooge to the Ghost. 'There he is! We were very good friends.'

'My boys!' said Fezziwig. 'No more work tonight! Christmas Eve, Dick! Christmas, Ebenezer! Let's close the shutters•!' cried old Fezziwig.

- **apprentice:** person working and learning how to do a job
- **cheerful:** happy
- **former self:** person (he) was when he was younger
- **rubbed his hands:** moved his hands together (usually when one is happy)
- **shutters:** wooden or metal covers on the outside of a window
- **warehouse:** large building to store goods in

43

The two young men ran into the street and closed the shutters.

'Clear everything away•, boys! Let's make room for the party!'

It was done in a minute. They washed the floor. They put coal on the fire, and soon the warehouse was the cosiest•, warmest, brightest• ballroom•. In came a fiddler• with a music book. In came Mrs Fezziwig, with a big smile on her face. In came the three pretty Miss Fezziwigs. In came the six young men whose hearts they broke. In came all Mr Fezziwig's employees. In they all came, one after another. And soon, there were twenty couples dancing round the room. There were dances, and there were games and more dances. And there was cake, and there was beef•, and there were mince pies and lots of beer. When the clock struck eleven, the party finished. Mr and Mrs Fezziwig stood by the door. They said goodbye to everybody as they left. And they wished them a Merry Christmas. For the whole time, Scrooge imagined he was in the scene with his former self. He remembered everything, and enjoyed everything.

'It was so easy,' said the Ghost, 'to make these people happy.'

'Easy?' repeated Scrooge.

The Ghost told Scrooge to listen to the two apprentices. They were praising• Fezziwig. And then he said, 'He has only spent a few pounds of your mortal money. Does he really deserve• all this praise?'

GLOSSARY

- **ballroom:** place to dance
- **beef:** meat from a cow
- **brightest:** with most light and life
- **clear away:** make space; tidy up
- **cosiest:** most comfortable and like home
- **deserve:** merit
- **fiddler:** person who plays the violin
- **praising:** saying nice things about

Scrooge was angry at the Ghost's remark•. 'It isn't about money, Ghost,' he said, speaking like the young Scrooge. 'He has the power• to make us happy or unhappy. He can make our work easy or difficult. The happiness he gives is worth a fortune in gold.' Then, suddenly, Scrooge stopped talking.

'What's the matter?' asked the Ghost.

'Nothing,' said Scrooge.

'There's something wrong,' the Ghost continued.

'No,' said Scrooge, 'No. I would like to be able to talk to my clerk now. That's all.'

As Scrooge spoke, his former self turned down• the lamps. And Scrooge and the Ghost stood side by side• in the open air.

'I haven't got much time left,' said the Ghost. 'Quick!'

Scrooge saw himself again. He was older now. And his face showed signs of greed•.

He was not alone. He was sitting by a pretty young girl. There were tears in her eyes.

'Belle,' Scrooge said quietly.

GLOSSARY

- **greed:** desire for more than you need
- **power:** ability; (here) possibility
- **remark:** words; what he said
- **side by side:** next to each other
- **turned down:** made the light less bright

46

'Another idol• has replaced• me,' Belle said, softly.

'What idol has replaced you?'

'A golden one,' replied Belle. 'I've seen you lose all your good ambitions•. And now all you are interested in is making money.'

BELLE

What is the relationship between Belle and Scrooge?
What is the idol that has replaced her?

- **ambitions:** goals; plans
- **idol:** person or thing that is loved and admired; false god
- **replaced:** substituted; taken the place of

'So what?•' he replied. 'My feelings haven't changed towards you.'

Belle shook her head.

'Have they?'

'When we met, we were both poor,' said Belle. 'And we were happy to be poor for a while. When we met, you were another man.'

'I was a boy,' he said impatiently•.

'You know that you've changed,' Belle replied. 'We can't make each other happy any more. I've thought about this a lot. You don't have to marry me.'

'Have I ever said that I don't want to marry you?'

'Not in words,' Belle replied.

'In what, then?'

'You're not the same person,' said Belle. 'Would you try to win my heart• now? I don't think so! You wouldn't choose to marry a poor girl like me now. And so, I release• you from your promise.'

He was about to speak, but Belle continued, 'I hope you'll be happy!' Then she stood up, and they said goodbye to each other.

GLOSSARY

- **impatiently:** unable to wait
- **release:** set free; let go
- **So what?:** That's not important
- **win my heart:** make me love you

'Ghost!' said Scrooge, 'Don't show me any more! Take me home.'

'One shadow more!' said the Ghost.

'No more!' cried Scrooge. 'I don't want to see it. Don't show me any more!'

But the Ghost held him and made him look.

They were in another room. It was not very large, but it was very comfortable. A beautiful young girl sat by the fire. She looked so like Belle that Scrooge thought it was her. Then he saw Belle. She was now an attractive• woman, and she was sitting opposite her daughter. They were laughing happily. The room was very noisy. There were more children than Scrooge could count.

Just then, there was a knock at the door, and everybody ran towards it. The father came in. He was carrying lots of Christmas toys and presents. With shrieks• of happiness, the children dived into• his pockets to steal• his brown-paper packages•. Their happiness was indescribable•. Then, one by one, the children left the room.

And they climbed to the top of the house, and went to bed. And now Scrooge saw the master of the house, sitting happily with his daughter and her mother by the fire. *She could be my daughter,* he thought, and his eyes filled with tears.

- **attractive:** pretty; good-looking
- **dived into:** put their hands in quickly
- **indescribable:** (here) very strong
- **packages:** parcels; presents
- **shrieks:** loud cries
- **steal:** take without asking

'Ghost,' said Scrooge in a sad voice, 'take me away from this place. I can't bear it•!'

He turned to the Ghost. It looked down at him. And he saw pieces of all the faces from his past in its face. The Ghost's light was very bright. Scrooge grabbed• the cap and quickly pressed it down on the Ghost's head.

But although Scrooge pressed• the cap down with all his strength, he could not hide the light.

Scrooge felt very tired. He gave the cap one last squeeze•. Then his hand relaxed. He was in his bedroom now. Exhausted•, he got into bed, and fell asleep.

- **exhausted:** very tired
- **grabbed:** took quickly and suddenly
- **I can't bear it!:** It is too difficult for me!
- **pressed:** pushed hard
- **squeeze:** firm press with his hands

PART III: THE SECOND OF THE THREE GHOSTS

Scrooge woke up in the middle of a huge snore•. He sat up in bed. It was nearly one o'clock. He closed all the curtains round the bed. He didn't want this ghost to surprise him.

The clock struck one. Nothing came. Five minutes, ten minutes, a quarter of an hour went by, and nothing came. Scrooge lay on his bed, in a blaze• of red light. This was more frightening than ten ghosts. At last, he decided the ghostly red light was coming from the next room. So he got up quietly and went to the door.

The moment Scrooge put his hand on the door handle•, a strange voice told him to enter. He went in.

It was his room. But it was different. It looked like a forest. Holly and mistletoe hung from the walls and ceiling. And there was a big fire. There were turkeys, geese, chickens, beef, sausages, mince pies, red-hot chestnuts, rosy-red apples, juicy oranges, and huge Christmas puddings covering the floor. And on this throne• of food, there sat a jolly• giant• with a glowing• torch.•

'Come in!' said the Ghost. 'Come in!'

- **blaze:** flash
- **door handle:** part of a door that opens it
- **giant:** very large, tall person
- **glowing:** shining
- **jolly:** happy and laughing
- **snore:** loud noise made when asleep
- **throne:** chair that a king or queen sits on
- **torch:** long stick with fire on the end

Scrooge went in, timidly•. The Ghost's eyes were very kind. But Scrooge couldn't look at it.

'I am the Ghost of Christmas Present,' said the Ghost. 'Look at me!'

Scrooge looked at it. It wore a green robe•, bordered with• white fur•. Its feet were bare•. And it wore a holly wreath• on its head. It had long brown curly hair, a kind face, and a cheerful voice. The Ghost of Christmas Present stood up.

'Ghost,' said Scrooge, 'I didn't want to go out last night. But I learnt some valuable• lessons. Tonight, I am ready to follow you.'

'Touch my robe!' said the Ghost. Scrooge did as he was told.

Holly, mistletoe, turkeys, geese, chickens, meat, sausages, pies, puddings and fruit, all vanished•. So did the room, the fire, the red glow, and the night. They stood in the city streets on Christmas morning. It was very cold, and people were shovelling away• the snow from the pavement in front of their houses. They were happy. They called out to one another and threw snowballs.

THE GHOST'S ROBE

What happens when Scrooge touches the second ghost's robe?
Why does this happen?

GLOSSARY

- **bare:** without shoes or socks
- **bordered with:** with; at the edges
- **fur:** animal hair
- **robe:** long coat
- **shovelling away:** clearing
- **timidly:** nervously and shyly
- **valuable:** useful
- **vanished:** disappeared suddenly
- **wreath:** circle of flowers

Scrooge and the Ghost went straight to Scrooge's clerk's house. At the door, the Ghost smiled, and stopped to bless• Bob Cratchit's home with his torch.

They went in, and they saw Mrs Cratchit. She was laying the table•. Belinda Cratchit, her second eldest daughter, was helping her.

The two smaller Cratchits, a boy and a girl, came running in. 'We smelt our goose at the baker's,' they shouted, and they danced around the table.

'Where's your father?' said Mrs Cratchit. 'And your brother, Tiny Tim! And Martha wasn't as late as this last Christmas Day!'

GLOSSARY

- **bless:** ask for God's protection, happiness or good fortune
- **laying the table:** putting the knives and forks, etc. on the table

54

'Here I am, mother!' said a girl, in the doorway.

'You're very late!' said Mrs Cratchit, kissing her a dozen times•.

'We had a lot of work to finish last night,' replied the girl, 'and I had to clear up• this morning, Mother!'

'Well, never mind•! You're here now,' said Mrs Cratchit.

'Father's coming,' cried the two young Cratchits.

In came Bob Cratchit in his threadbare• clothes. Tiny Tim sat on his shoulder. Poor Tiny Tim! He couldn't walk without crutches•.

- **a dozen times:** many times (a dozen is twelve)
- **clear up:** tidy up and put things away
- **crutches:**
- **threadbare:** thin and old clothes
- **Well, never mind!:** Don't worry!

The two young Cratchits took Tiny Tim to the wash-house, to see the Christmas pudding.

'And how did little Tim behave• in church?' asked Mrs Cratchit.

'He was as good as gold•,' said Bob, 'but sometimes he says the strangest things. He said to me, on the way home, "I hope that everybody in church saw me because I'm disabled. I want them to remember this on Christmas Day. God made lame• beggars walk. And he made blind• men see".'

There was a tremor• in Bob Cratchit's voice when he told them this.

Tiny Tim hobbled• back into the room on his crutches. His brother and sister helped him. They helped him to sit on his stool by the fire.

Peter, and the two young Cratchits went to fetch• the goose from the baker's.

Such excitement followed. Mrs Cratchit made the gravy. Master Peter mashed• the potatoes. Miss Belinda sweetened• the apple sauce. Bob sat Tiny Tim at the table. Then, everybody sat down.

They ate the goose, the gravy•, the potatoes, and the apple sauce. Then Mrs Cratchit went to get the pudding.

GLOSSARY

- **behave:** act
- **blind:** not able to see
- **fetch:** get
- **good as gold:** very good
- **gravy:** sauce for meat
- **hobbled:** walked with difficulty
- **lame:** not able to walk correctly
- **mashed:** crushed; made smooth
- **sweetened:** added sugar
- **tremor:** shaking of one's body or voice

'Oh, it's a wonderful pudding!' Bob Cratchit said. Everybody said something about the pudding. But nobody said it was a small pudding for a large family.

At last, they finished dinner, and they all sat around the fire.

'A Merry Christmas to us all, my dears! God bless us!' said Bob Cratchit.

THE CRATCHITS

In pairs, think of words to describe the Cratchit family and their Christmas dinner.

'Yes, God bless us all!' said Tiny Tim. He sat very close to his father on his little stool. Bob held his thin little hand in his.

'Ghost,' said Scrooge. 'Will Tiny Tim live?'

'I see an empty stool,' replied the Ghost, 'and a crutch without an owner•. The child will die.'

'No, no!' said Scrooge. 'Oh no, kind Ghost! Say he will live!'

'He is weak•. Let him die. There are too many people in the world,' replied the Ghost.

Scrooge felt very ashamed• when he heard the ghost use his own• words.

SHAME

When did Scrooge use these words?
Why does he feel ashamed?

GLOSSARY

- **felt ashamed:** felt sorry and bad about past actions or words
- **own:** his
- **owner:** person to whom something belongs
- **weak:** not strong

'It may be that in the sight of God, you are more worthless• and less fit• to live than millions like Tiny Tim,' said the Ghost.

Scrooge trembled at the Ghost's rebuke•, and looked at the ground. But he raised his head quickly when he heard his own name.

'Mr Scrooge!' said Bob. 'Let's drink to Mr Scrooge, the founder• of the feast•!'

'The founder of the feast!' cried Mrs Cratchit. 'He's a horrible mean old man.'

'My dear!' said Bob. 'The children! Christmas Day.'

'I'll drink to his health for your sake•, not for his,' said Mrs Cratchit. 'Long life to him! A Merry Christmas and a Happy New Year! He'll be very merry and very happy. I'm sure!'

By this time, it was getting dark, and it was snowing heavily. As Scrooge and the Ghost moved along the streets, the generous Ghost poured• happiness on everything!

- **less fit to:** not good enough to
- **feast:** big meal
- **for your sake:** for you; for your good
- **founder:** person responsible for; creator
- **poured:** (here) gave a lot
- **rebuke:** criticism; words against someone
- **worthless:** useless

Then suddenly, Scrooge heard a laugh. He was surprised when he recognised the laugh. It was his nephew's! Scrooge was now standing in a bright room with the Ghost.

'Ha, ha, ha, ha!' laughed Scrooge's nephew. 'Ha, ha, ha, ha!'

When Scrooge's nephew laughed, his wife laughed, and all their friends laughed, too.

'Ha, ha! Ha, ha, ha, ha!'

'He said that Christmas was a humbug!' cried Scrooge's nephew. 'He believed it, too!'

'Shame on him•, Fred!' said his pretty wife, indignantly•.

'He's a funny old fellow•,' said Scrooge's nephew, 'and he could be nicer. However, he only hurts himself. I feel sorry for him. I can't be angry with him.'

'Don't feel sorry for him, Fred,' said his wife. 'He's very rich!'

'So what, my dear!' said Scrooge's nephew. 'His wealth• is no use to him. He doesn't do any good with it. Come on! Let's play a game!'

GLOSSARY

• **fellow:** man
• **indignantly:** shocked and angrily

• **Shame on him!:** He should feel sorry for what he has done or said
• **wealth:** money; riches

And so they played "How, When and Where?". There were about twenty people there, young and old. They all played, and so did Scrooge. He was really enjoying himself. He forgot that they couldn't hear him. He shouted out his guesses•. And very often he was right.

The Ghost was happy to see him in this mood•. Scrooge didn't want to leave.

THE NEPHEW'S HOUSE

What does Scrooge's nephew think of him?
How is Scrooge changing?
What are the ghost's feelings?

• **guesses:** (here) answers without knowing they are correct

• **mood:** way one feels

'We have to go now,' said the Ghost. Then the whole scene disappeared. Scrooge and the Ghost were on their travels again.

They visited many homes. The Ghost made sick people well again, and poor people rich. They visited workhouses, hospitals and prisons. The Ghost left happiness in all of them. And he taught Scrooge to do the same. It was a long night. Scrooge noticed that the Ghost was getting older and older.

'Are ghosts' lives really this short?' asked Scrooge.

'My life on this Earth is very short,' replied the Ghost. 'It ends tonight.'

'Tonight!' cried Scrooge.

'Tonight at midnight. Listen! It's nearly midnight.'

'Forgive● me for asking,' said Scrooge. He was looking at the Ghost's robe. 'But what's that? Is it a foot or a claw●?'

GLOSSARY

● **claw:** hard nails on the foot of a bird or animal

● **forgive:** pardon

The Ghost lifted its robe, and Scrooge saw two miserable children. They knelt• at the Ghost's feet and clung• to its robe.

There was a boy and a girl. They were thin and scowling•. They were young, but their faces looked old. No monster could be more frightening than these two children.

Scrooge stepped back. 'Ghost, are they yours?' He asked.

'They are Man's,' said the Ghost. 'This boy is Ignorance•. This girl is Want•. Beware• of them both. But most of all, beware of this boy.'

'Do they not have a home to go to?' cried Scrooge.

'Are there no prisons?' said the Ghost. 'Are there no workhouses?'

The clock struck twelve.

IGNORANCE AND WANT

During his life Charles Dickens campaigned• for education for everyone. Here he is telling the reader to beware of 'Ignorance' (no education) and 'Want' (poverty). And to give everyone an education so that they don't have to be poor.

What things do you think we should campaign for in our society?

- **beware:** be careful (in case of danger)
- **campaigned:** (here) worked to make people aware of something
- **clung:** held very tightly
- **ignorance:** no education or morals
- **knelt:** sat on their knees on the floor
- **scowling:** with an angry expression
- **want:** poverty

Scrooge looked around him for the Ghost, but he couldn't see it. Then he remembered old Jacob Marley's prediction•. He lifted his eyes, and he saw a solemn• Ghost. It was hooded•, and it was moving like a mist along the ground, towards him.

e. ONLINE ACTIVITIES • Part 3

PART IV: THE LAST OF THE THREE GHOSTS

The Ghost moved slowly and silently towards him. And as it moved through the air, it scattered• gloom•.

The Ghost wore a black robe. The robe covered its head, its face, and its body. The only thing visible was a hand. The Ghost neither spoke nor moved. Scrooge was terrified•.

'Are you the Ghost of Christmas Yet To Come•?' asked Scrooge.

The Ghost didn't answer, but it pointed its hand in front of it.

'You are going to show me the future,' Scrooge continued. 'Am I right, Ghost?'

The Ghost nodded• its head. That was the only answer Scrooge received.

GLOSSARY

- **gloom:** sadness
- **hooded:** with a covering on its head
- **Lead on!:** Show me the way
- **nodded:** moved as if to say "yes"
- **prediction:** what he thinks will happen in the future
- **scattered:** threw/spread over a large area
- **solemn:** serious and unhappy-looking
- **terrified:** very frightened
- **yet to come:** in the future

'Ghost of the Future,' he said, 'I am more afraid of you than of all the other ghosts. But because I want to be a better man, I will go with you. Please, speak to me!'

It didn't reply. The hand pointed straight in front of them.

'Lead on!•' said Scrooge.

The Ghost moved forwards. Scrooge followed in the shadow of its robe. And the robe carried him along. The city sprang up• around them. There they were, in the heart of• it. The Ghost stopped beside some businessmen at the Stock Exchange•. His hand was pointing to them, so Scrooge listened to their conversation.

'I only know he's dead,' said a great fat man.

'When did he die?' asked another.

'Last night, I think.'

'What was the matter with him?' asked a third.

'God knows•,' said the first, with a yawn•.

'What has he done with his money?' asked a red-faced gentleman.

'I don't know,' said the great fat man, yawning again. 'He hasn't left it to me. That's all I know.'

Everybody laughed.

'It will be a very small funeral,' said the great fat man. 'I don't think anybody will go to it.'

GLOSSARY

- **God knows:** I really don't know
- **in the heart of:** at the centre of
- **sprang up:** appeared suddenly
- **Stock Exchange**: the place where people buy and sell stocks and shares
- **yawn:** act of opening the mouth very wide as if bored or sleepy

Scrooge knew the men. And he looked towards the Ghost for an explanation. He didn't understand why this conversation was important. But he knew it must be.

Scrooge looked around the place. He looked at the clock. It was strange. He was usually there at this time, but he couldn't see himself.

THE DEAD MAN

Who do you think the dead man is? What are the men's feelings for the dead man? Was he a good friend of theirs? What are the qualities of a good friend? In pairs, make a list.

They left the Stock Exchange. And they went to an area of the city that Scrooge never went to. The streets were dark and dirty. The shops and houses were rundown. The whole neighbourhood smelt of crime•, dirt, and sadness. Finally, they came to a shop. It sold iron•, old rags•, bottles and bones. An old grey-haired man was sitting in the shop. He was smoking his pipe•.

Just then a woman with a heavy bundle• came into the shop. She threw her bundle on the floor.

'What have you got for me then, Mrs Dilber?' asked the man.

'Open the bundle, Joe,' she said.

'What are these?' asked the old man. 'Bed curtains?'

'Yes, bed curtains!'

'Did you take them down with the dead man lying there?' asked Joe.

'Yes,' replied the woman. 'Why not? He was all alone. There was nobody crying for him.'

Scrooge listened to this conversation in horror•. 'Ghost!' said Scrooge, trembling from head to foot. 'I understand. This unhappy man could be me. My life is going in that direction now. Oh no! Where are we now?'

GLOSSARY

- **bundle:** several things tied together
- **crime:** illegal activity
- **in horror:** in shock
- **iron:** strong metal
- **pipe:**
- **rags:** pieces of old clothes

68

They were in a bedroom now. It was dark and miserable. There was an uncurtained• bed. And on the bed, under an old sheet•, there lay a body. Scrooge looked at the Ghost. Its hand pointed to the bed. Scrooge looked at it, but he couldn't lift the sheet and look at the dead man's face.

'Ghost!' said Scrooge. 'This is a terrible• place. I've learnt my lesson•. Let's go!'

The Ghost was still pointing to the bed.

'I understand you,' Scrooge said, 'but I can't lift the sheet. Please, Ghost! Show me a tender• death scene, or the memory of this dark room will stay with me forever.'

- **I've learnt my lesson:** I understand my mistakes
- **sheet:** cloth for a bed
- **tender:** showing kind and gentle feelings
- **terrible:** very bad
- **uncurtained:** without curtains

The Ghost led him through several familiar• streets to poor Bob Cratchit's house, and they found Mrs Cratchit and the children sitting around the fire.

It was very quiet. The noisy little Cratchits sat as still as statues• in one corner. Mrs Cratchit and her daughters were sewing•. But why were they so quiet?

'Oh, poor Tiny Tim!' said one.

'Your father will be home soon,' said Mrs Cratchit.

'He walks more slowly than he used to, Mother,' said Peter.

They were very quiet again. Then Mrs Cratchit said, in a falsely• cheerful voice, 'He used to walk very fast with Tiny Tim on his shoulder. Oh, your father loved that boy so much.'

GLOSSARY

• **as still as statues:** without moving
• **falsely:** (here) not with real feelings
• **familiar:** thing or person one recognises or knows well well
• **sewing:** making or repairing clothes

70

Just then the door opened. 'Ah, here's your father!' said Mrs Cratchit. And she hurried over to greet● him. His tea was ready for him on the hob●. He sat down. The two young Cratchits got on his knees and hugged● him, as if to say, *Don't be upset, Father.*

'Did you go to the graveyard● today, again, Robert?' said his wife.

'Yes, my dear,' replied Bob. 'I promised him. My little, little child!' wept Bob. 'My little child!'

Then the scene faded away●.

'Ghost,' said Scrooge, 'I think you are about to leave me. But first, please tell me. Who was that dead man?'

The Ghost of Christmas Yet To Come took him to a very familiar place.

'This is where I used to work,' said Scrooge. 'There's my office. Let me see myself!'

The Ghost stopped. The hand pointed in a different direction.

'My office is here,' said Scrooge. 'Why are you pointing over there?'

The hand continued to point in the other direction. Quickly, Scrooge looked through his office window. It was still an office, but it was not his. The furniture was not the same, and the man in the chair was not him.

- **faded away:** disappeared slowly
- **graveyard:** area of land near a church where dead people are buried
- **greet:** welcome; say hello to
- **hob:** top of a cooker where one heats and cooks food
- **hugged:** put their arms around

He followed the Ghost to an iron gate. It was a graveyard. The Ghost stood among the graves•, and pointed down to one. Scrooge walked towards it trembling. He read the name on the neglected• stone of the neglected grave. It was his name, EBENEZER SCROOGE.

'Am I that man on the bed?' he cried.

The finger pointed from the grave to him, and back again.

'No, Ghost! Oh no, no!'

The finger was still there.

'Ghost!' he cried. 'Listen to me! I am not the man I was. I will be a different man! Why are you showing me this?'

For the first time, the hand trembled.

'Good Ghost,' he continued. And he knelt on the ground before it. 'Tell me that I can change these shadows!'

The hand trembled again.

GLOSSARY_____

- **graves:** place in the ground where dead people are buried

- **neglected:** not given enough care or attention

'I will celebrate Christmas and try to keep it all year. I will not forget your lessons. Oh, tell me I can wash away the writing on this stone!'

Scrooge caught the Ghost's hand. He begged the Ghost to change his fate. But then he saw the Ghost's hood and robe shrink•. Then it disappeared into the bedpost•.

PART V: THE END OF THE STORY

YES! It was his bed. It was his room. Now he could put things right!• Scrooge jumped out of bed. 'Oh Jacob Marley, thank you!'

'They are still here!' cried Scrooge, holding one of his bed curtains in his arms. 'They are here – I am here! Now, I can change the future. I know I can!'

Scrooge hurried to get dressed. And in his excitement, he put on his vest inside out. He put on his trousers upside down•. He tore• his shirt. And he couldn't find his socks.

- **bedpost:** wooden part of a bed
- **put things right:** correct his mistakes
- **shrink:** get smaller
- **tore:** made a hole in
- **upside down:** the bottom part first (not the correct way)

'A Merry Christmas to everybody!' shouted Scrooge. 'A Happy New Year to all the world!'

He stopped when he heard the church bells• ringing. He ran and opened the window. No fog. It was a clear, cold day. Golden sunlight! Sweet, fresh air! Happy bells! What a wonderful, wonderful day!

'What day is it today?' cried Scrooge, calling down to a boy in his Sunday clothes.

'EH?' replied the boy.

'What day is it today?' repeated Scrooge.

'Today?' replied the boy. 'It's CHRISTMAS DAY!'

GLOSSARY

• bells:

Happy, Scrooge called down to the boy. 'Do you know the butcher's, on the corner?'

'Of course!' replied the boy.

'Good!' said Scrooge. 'Have they sold the big prize turkey in the window?'

'What, the one as big as me?' replied the boy.

'Yes!' said Scrooge.

'It's still there,' replied the boy.

'Is it?' said Scrooge. 'Then go and buy it. I'll give you a shilling.'

'I'll send it to Bob Cratchit's!' said Scrooge.

• **prize:** (here) the best

After that, Scrooge put on his best suit•, and then he was ready to go out. Once outside, Scrooge smiled at everybody, and two or three people said, 'Good morning, sir! A Merry Christmas to you!' He was walking along the street, when he saw one of the kind old gentlemen from the day before. He felt very embarrassed. But he greeted him.

'My dear sir,' said Scrooge, shaking the gentleman's hand. 'How do you do?•'

'Mr Scrooge?'

'Yes,' said Scrooge. 'Please forgive me for my behaviour• yesterday. And will you...' Scrooge whispered• something in his ear.

'Good heavens!' cried the gentleman. 'My dear Mr Scrooge, are you serious?'

'Of course,' said Scrooge. 'Not a penny less. It includes a lot of back-payments•.'

'My dear sir,' said the gentleman. 'That's very kind of you!'

'Come and see me sometime,' said Scrooge.

'I will!' cried the old gentleman.

'Thank you,' said Scrooge.

GLOSSARY

- **back-payments:** money owing from the past
- **behaviour:** actions
- **How do you do?:** formal greeting
- **suit:** jacket and trousers of the same cloth
- **whispered:** said very quietly

That afternoon, Scrooge walked to his nephew's house. He was very nervous. He walked past the door several times before he finally knocked on it.

The door opened. 'Merry Christmas, Fred!' said Scrooge. 'I have come for dinner. Can I come in?'

Fred was very happy to see Scrooge. Everything was the same. It was a wonderful party.

The next morning, Scrooge went to the office early. He wanted to get there before Bob. The clock struck nine. No Bob. A quarter past. No Bob. He was eighteen and a half minutes late.

Scrooge sat with his door wide open, so he could see Bob come in. Bob took his hat and scarf off before he opened the door. Then he ran to his stool. He quickly sat down and started writing very fast with his pen.

'Hello!' growled● Scrooge, in his old voice. 'You're late.'

'I'm very sorry, sir,' said Bob.

'Come here,' said Scrooge.

'It's only once a year, sir!' pleaded Bob. 'It won't happen again!'

'Now, listen to me,' said Scrooge. 'I'm going to give you a pay rise●! And I'm going to help your family. A Merry Christmas, Bob!'

Scrooge kept his word. He helped Bob's family. Tiny Tim did NOT die. And Scrooge was a second father to him. Scrooge became as good a friend, as good a boss, and as good a man, as the good old city knew, or any other good old city or town, or country, in the good old world.

He never saw the Ghosts again. And people always said, 'Mr Scrooge knows how to celebrate Christmas better than any other man on Earth!' May somebody say that about us, too. All of us!

And so, as Tiny Tim said,
God bless us all!

GLOSSARY

- **growled:** said in a cross voice
- **pay rise:** more money every month; a higher salary

AFTER READING TALK ABOUT THE STORY

1 **Read each sentence and circle the number that is most true for you.**

> **1** = Not really   **5** = Definitely

a I liked the story.
1   **2**   **3**   **4**   **5**

b I had no problems understanding the story.
1   **2**   **3**   **4**   **5**

c I have learnt new words.
1   **2**   **3**   **4**   **5**

d I would recommend the book to a friend.
1   **2**   **3**   **4**   **5**

2 **The ghosts visited Scrooge to teach him a lesson. What did Scrooge learn from them? And what can we learn from them?**

3 **There are a lot of sad scenes in *A Christmas Carol*. In your opinion, which is the saddest scene and why?**

4 **Did the story have a happy or an unhappy ending?**

5 **What happened to the following characters at the end of the story?**
   a Tiny Tim
   b Bob Cratchit
   c Scrooge

AFTER READING COMPREHENSION

1 Are the following sentences true (T) or false (F)? Tick (✓).

		T	F
a	Marley wasn't dead at the beginning of the story.	☐	☐
b	Scrooge's nephew thinks Christmas is a time to be generous and kind.	☐	☐
c	Poor people were happy to go and stay in the workhouses.	☐	☐
d	When Marley was alive, he didn't help the poor.	☐	☐
e	The Ghost of Christmas Past never gets old.	☐	☐
f	Mr Fezziwig was very kind to his employees.	☐	☐
g	Money was more important to the young Scrooge than Belle.	☐	☐
h	Scrooge was happy because he didn't marry Belle.	☐	☐
i	The Ghost of Christmas Present shows Scrooge a grave.	☐	☐
j	Scrooge doesn't want Tiny Tim to die.	☐	☐
k	Scrooge didn't enjoy seeing the party at his nephew's house.	☐	☐
l	The Ghost of Christmas Future never speaks.	☐	☐
m	Scrooge realises he doesn't want to die a sad and lonely man.	☐	☐
n	In the end, Scrooge becomes very generous and helps Bob Cratchit.	☐	☐

2 **Match the two halves of the sentences to sum up the story.**

a ☐	At the beginning of the story Scrooge is	**1** and teach him a lesson.
b ☐	His dead partner, Jacob Marley, visits him	**2** his unhappy life and the mistakes he has made.
c ☐	Three ghosts haunt him	**3** a mean, miserable, rich old man.
d ☐	The three ghosts show him	**4** and his kindness saves Tiny Tim's life.
e ☐	In the end, Scrooge changes	**5** and warns him to be kind and to help people.

3 **When does Scrooge say or think the following? Match.**

A There was a boy singing a Christmas carol at my door last night. I would like to give him some money.

B I would like to be able to talk to my clerk now.

C She could be my daughter.

F Oh no, kind Ghost! Say he will live!

E I understand. This unhappy man could be me.

D I am not the man I was. I will be a different man!

At the visit to

1 ☐ Bob Cratchit's on Christmas Day

2 ☐ the shop

3 ☐ the graveyard

4 ☐ Mr Fezziwig's warehouse where Scrooge worked

5 ☐ Belle's house

6 ☐ Scrooge's old school

AFTER READING CHARACTERS

1 **Match the adjectives to the characters. Then write short descriptions of each character using the words.**

> mean   cheerful   powerful speaker
> disabled   miserable   cross   weak
> warm-hearted   as good as gold

Tiny Tim	Scrooge	Scrooge's nephew
....	....	....
....	....	....
....	....	....

2 **Replace the words in red in the description of Scrooge with the correct words from the box below.**

> harsh   frost   froze   blue
> thaw   pointed   iced   mean

Scrooge was a cold, greedy, **(a)** generous .... old man! The cold within him **(b)** warmed .... his old face. It made his eyes red, and his thin lips **(c)** pink .... And it spoke out in his **(d)** kind .... voice. A **(e)** cloth .... covered his head, his eyebrows, and his **(f)** round .... chin. He **(g)** warmed .... his office, and he didn't **(h)** cool .... it one degree at Christmas.

3 **Who is your favourite character in *A Christmas Carol*? Write a paragraph about him or her.**

4 Tick (✓) true (T) or false (F) next to the statements about the three ghosts.

The Ghost of Christmas Past

		T	F
a	It was no taller than a child.	☐	☐
b	It looked like an old man.	☐	☐
c	A light shone from the top of its head.	☐	☐
d	It wore a green dress.	☐	☐
e	Scrooge saw faces from his past in the Ghost's face.	☐	☐

The Ghost of Christmas Present

		T	F
f	It was very cheerful.	☐	☐
g	It was very short.	☐	☐
h	It held a torch.	☐	☐
i	It had cruel eyes.	☐	☐
j	It sprinkled happiness on everyone and everything.	☐	☐

The Ghost of Christmas Yet to Come

		T	F
k	It was very serious.	☐	☐
l	It wore a white robe.	☐	☐
m	Scrooge couldn't see its face.	☐	☐
n	It told him lots of things.	☐	☐
o	Scrooge could only see its hand.	☐	☐

5 Which ghost do you think is the most frightening and why?

AFTER READING VOCABULARY

1 Use five of the words in the box to complete the sentences.

> waistcoat   yawn   beggar   lame
> wide   nod   shame   sheet

a If you .... your head, it means you move it as if to say 'yes'.

b .... open means completely open.

c A jacket without sleeves is called a ....

d A .... is a poor person who asks for money or food.

e '............... on you! You should be very sorry for what you have done!'

2 Complete the word formation table below.

ADJECTIVE	NOUN
SAD	*SADNESS*
....	GREED
COLD	....
....	WOOL
CHARITABLE	....
....	GLOOM
GLOWING	....
....	WOOD
BLIND	....
....	POWER
DIRTY	....

3 💬 **Make sentences with a partner with the words you find in Exercise 2.**

4 **Complete the following sentences with the correct question tags.**

Example: *'You don't mean that, do you?'*

a 'Marley died seven years ago, ... ?'

b 'Workhouses are still in operation, ... ?'

c 'I'm different today, ... ?'

d 'You've been dead for seven years, ... ?'

e 'We had a lot of work to finish, ... ?'

f 'You will be a different man, ... ?'

g 'You won't forget my lesson, ... ?'

h 'Scrooge could be nicer, ... ?'

i 'He hasn't left the money to me, ... ?'

5 *Who, that, which,* **or** *whose*? **Choose the correct relative pronoun.**

a Scrooge and the Ghost went straight to Scrooge's clerk's house, ... was in Camden Town.

b In came Bob Cratchit, ... was in his threadbare clothes.

c The man .... Scrooge worked with was called Marley.

d Scrooge hated anyone .... celebrated Christmas.

e Bob Cratchit earned fifteen shillings a week, ... was very little.

f Scrooge kept an eye on his clerk, ... name was Bob Cratchit.

g All three Ghosts seemed to say that it is love .... really matters, not money.

AFTER READING PLOT AND THEME

1 Which comes first? Put the events in the right order.

1	2	3	4	5	6	7	8	9	10	11	12	13	14	15	16	17
a																g

a We learn from the narrator that Jacob Marley is dead.

b The Ghost of Christmas Present comes to haunt Scrooge.

c Scrooge's former fiancée, Belle, tells him that she doesn't want to marry him.

d We learn that Scrooge hates Christmas. And he refuses his nephew's invitation to dinner on Christmas Day.

e Scrooge visits his old school and sees himself as a boy.

f Scrooge watches his nephew's Christmas party and sees everyone having fun.

g Scrooge learns that Tiny Tim is dead.

h Scrooge sees Belle with her beautiful daughter and family celebrating Christmas.

i Scrooge learns that Tiny Tim will die.

j Scrooge overhears a conversation about a man's death. Nobody is mourning his death.

k The Ghost of Christmas Past comes to haunt Scrooge.

l Scrooge learns that he is the dead man and that he died alone.

m Scrooge visits his clerk Bob Cratchit's house on Christmas Day.

n Scrooge visits his former workplace at Christmas and sees his kind boss, Mr Fezziwig.

o The Ghost of Marley visits Scrooge and warns him to be kinder and more generous.

p The Ghost of Christmas Yet to Come haunts Scrooge.

q Scrooge wakes up.

2 💬 **What are the themes of the story? In pairs, write a list. Then discuss them in groups.**

3 💬 **What is the story's message about Christmas? Discuss in groups.**

4 **What do you think Dickens means in his introduction to the story, *"I have tried to write a ghost story that won't make you unhappy with yourselves, with each other, with the season, or with me. I hope it haunts your houses pleasantly."***
💬 **Discuss ideas in pairs.**

5 **At the end of the story, the narrator says, *"Mr Scrooge knows how to celebrate Christmas better than any other man on Earth!"* What would you do to give people the best Christmas on Earth? Write your plans for the best Christmas on Earth.**

K **A2 Key English Test Reading and Writing Part 4**

1 **For each sentence, choose the correct answer (A, B, or C).**

1 She looked so like Belle that Scrooge thought ..... was her.

   A it   **B** is   **C** that

2 Scrooge felt very ashamed when he heard the ghost use his ..... words.

   A own   **B** only   **C** last

3 – 'Do you believe in me or not?' asked the Ghost.
   – 'I do!' said Scrooge. 'I .....!'

   A had   **B** must   **C** need

4 The cold within Scrooge ..... his eyes red, and his thin lips blue.

   A made   **B** had   **C** did

5 Scrooge wanted to ..... his eye on his clerk, Bob Cratchit.

   A put   **B** have   **C** keep

6 'At Christmas time,' said the gentleman, 'we ..... give to the poor.'

   A should   **B** do   **C** won't

7 'We don't think that workhouses do ..... for people.'

   A lot   **B** enough   **C** something

8 'Now all you are interested ..... is making money.'

   A in   **B** to   **C** at

9 Poor Tiny Tim! He ..... walk without crutches.

   A couldn't   **B** must   **C** should

K A2 Key English Test Reading and Writing Part 5

2 Complete the text below about Dickens by writing ONE word for each gap.

Dickens's origins were middle class, but he experienced poverty first hand when his father was arrested and imprisoned for bankruptcy. He had to leave school, and at the **(1)** .... of twelve, he was sent to work in a factory, **(2)** .... he had to put labels on shoe polish bottles. Scholars **(3)** .... biographers agree that this personal experience of hardship, neglect and poverty when he was a child was a key factor in shaping Dickens's worldview, and it served as the basis for his books. This is **(4)** .... his novels are full of orphans and poor children. It is **(5)** .... he was one himself. Dickens never forgot the suffering he had to go through during **(6)** .... childhood. He knew **(7)** .... it was like to be alone and hungry and he wanted his readers to know it, **(8)** ....

K A2 Key English Test Writing Part 6

3 Bob Cratchit is amazed at Scrooge's new attitude towards Christmas and life in general. When he goes home after work, he decides to write a short letter to Scrooge's nephew to inform him about it. Write his message using 25 words or more.

4 Imagine you are a member of the charitable organisation who sent the two gentlemen to collect money for the poor at Christmas time. Write a report on the visit to Mr Scrooge. Write what happened during the visit using 25 words or more.

AFTER READING EXIT TEST

 1 **K Listen and tick (✓) the correct picture.**

1 a ☐   b ☐   c ☐

2 a ☐   b ☐   c ☐

3 a ☐   b ☐   c ☐

4 a ☐   b ☐   c ☐

5 a ☐   b ☐   c ☐

2 🄺 **Read the sentences about the story and choose the correct answer (1, 2 or 3) for each gap.**

a The story takes place in 19th century London in ....
  1 winter   **2** spring   **3** summer

b The main character is a very wealthy, mean, ... old man.
  1 cheerful   **2** miserable   **3** generous

c After Marley, he is visited by .... ghosts. Their visits make him a better man.
  1 five   **2** three   **3** four

d The ghosts make Scrooge .... his words and his actions.
  1 ashamed of   **2** angry about   **3** proud of

e After the ghosts' visits, Scrooge gives his clerk, Bob Cratchit, a ....
  1 package   **2** pay rise   **3** holiday

f Scrooge learns how to .... Christmas.
  1 celebrate   **2** ignore   **3** work at

3 💬 🄺 **Turn to page 52 and look at the picture of the Ghost of Christmas Present on his throne of food. Ask and answer questions about the picture.**

Is the ghost happy or sad?

It's happy.

Is the ghost frightening?

No, it isn't.

AFTER READING PROJECT

1 💬 **Be a good person.**
Talk about the qualities of a
good friend, a good teacher, a good parent and a good brother/
sister. Collect adjectives and write them in the table.

A good friend	A good teacher	A good parent	A good brother/sister
....	....	....	....
....	....	....	....
....	....	....	....
....	....	....	....

2 Be a better person.
Choose one of the writing tasks below.

a Imagine that you meet the Ghost of Christmas Past. What does it say to you? Think about things you did in the past. Is there anything you are not proud of? Is there a lesson you can learn from your past? Write a letter to yourself in the name of the Ghost of Christmas Past.

b Imagine that you meet the Ghost of Christmas Present. What problems in your school and town would you like the Ghost to make better? Is there anyone you can help? How can you make your environment better?

c Imagine you meet the Ghost of Christmas Yet To Come. Write a list of things you can do at Christmas in the future. How can you make people happier around you? What can you change for next Christmas?